The Soul Collection

Felt everything, wrote everyone

Kanika Sangeeta Shailendra Barfa

BookLeaf Publishing
India | USA | UK

Made with ❤ on the BookLeaf Publishing Platform
www.bookleafpub.in
www.bookleafpub.com

Dedication

Maa and Papa

For your unshaken faith, midnight prayers, and quiet sacrifices.

This book is my tribute to dreams we dreamed together—
yours that paused for me,
mine that bloomed because of you.

Preface

I never imagined that the quiet hobby I carried in my notebook would one day find its way into a book. Writing was never a grand plan—it was simply something that brought me peace, clarity, and joy.

This book is not a reflection of my journey, but a tribute to everyone else's. To those who've fought silent battles, chased impossible dreams, laughed through their struggles, or held on when letting go seemed easier—these poems are for you.

Each poem is a window into something raw,real and restless.Each page is a mirror, not of me, but of emotions we all feel—hope, doubt, strength, healing, ambition, love, and wonder.

This book began not just with pen and paper, but with a passion I inherited from my father—a writer himself.

If even a single poem makes someone feel seen, understood, or uplifted, then this book has served its purpose.

With all my heart

kanika

Preface

Acknowledgements

To my parents and grandparents- You gave me roots and wings , And Your belief became my backbone.

To my elder brother– I've never done anything without you, and yet here I am–doing this, for you, by myself.

To my entire family– Your pride and quiet love live in every line. You have all carried me further than you know. Though I couldn't mention each name.

To Somi my little sunshine- Everyone I love holds a piece of this book, but you carry my whole heart and book..

To all mentor and entrance journey- Thank you for the resilience you built in me through every setback.

To my friends– You know who you are. I may not name each of you here, but your love, and faith in me shaped this journey.

You all believed in me when I stopped believing in myself.

You encouraged me to turn this quiet passion into something worthy, this book also exists because of you guys.

This book may have been written by me, but it was built by all of you.

With all my heart,
Kanika

1. The Stage Called Life

We're all actors in our own little play,
Trying to mean something day by day.

Some wear masks, some wear none,
Some run away, some just run.

They told me life is about a job, a name,
But I think it's about staying sane.

About laughing so hard your ribs ache,
And dancing just for the joy you make.

It's about late talks and early sun,
About forgiving when the pain's not done.

It's not just success or a fancy role—
It's who you love and how you hold your soul.

So I'll keep acting in my imperfect scene,
With flaws, with dreams, with things unseen.

And maybe, just maybe, when the curtain falls—
I'll know I gave it my all.

2. Unsent Prayers

She folded her hands but said no word,
Her silence louder than prayers heard.

She'd grown too tired to kneel again,
Tired of asking and hiding pain.

There was a time she used to pray
For sunshine in her stormy day,

For love that didn't walk away,
For strength when life led her astray.

But years went by, her hope grew thin,
She stopped confessing what's within.

No temple bell or sacred light
Could ease the weight she held at night.

Yet somewhere in her quiet mind,
A softer voice, a faith confined,

Said maybe prayers don't need a sound—
Maybe they rise from broken ground.

So now she walks with head held high,
Still no answers, but she tries.

For not all faith is found in air—
Some grow in silence, like a prayer.

3. You Don't Need To Be Okay (Today)

It's okay if you cried last night,
If your chest still feels a little too tight.

If your smile is tired, and your heart unsure,
Healing isn't fast–it's slow and pure.

You don't have to glow every day,
You can just breathe, and that's okay.

Some days you bloom,
some days you break,

Both are needed,
For growth to take.

So stop being hard on yourself tonight,
You're trying, you're learning, you'll be alright.

The sun also hides before it shines—
You're not behind,
you're just in time.

4. Loved In Silence

He sat behind her every day,
In rows she never turned,

And carried words he never said,
In letters never burned

.

She spoke of someone else she liked,
With stars inside her grin—

He nodded like it didn't hurt,
Though something broke within.

He saved her photos quietly,
Liked posts without a trace—

And lived with what he couldn't say
Each time he saw her face.

Some boys don't write their love in poems,
Or whisper it at all—

They just love you from afar,
And catch you when you fall.

5. He Never Said It Loud

He passed her pen when hers went dry,
He stood behind when crowds ran by.

He saved the seat in every class,
Yet never let those moments pass.

He knew her laugh, her favorite song,
The way she cried when days felt long.

But never once did he confess,
He wore his love in quietness.

And though she never truly knew—
He cheered for her in all she'd do.

Love doesn't always need a name—
Some hearts just love without a claim.

And in his silence, bold and true—
He loved her more than words could do.

6. Small Town Heart

Came from a place where people wave,
Where silence lives and hearts behave.

Now you walk these city streets,
Among fast cars and louder beats.

Back home, stars were easy to see,
Here, lights glow but don't feel free.

Crowds don't smile, and nights feel cold,
Dreams are big, but hearts less bold.

Still you walk, still you try,
With dust on shoes and head held high.

This city's wild, but so are you—
you came to rise, not just get by.

7. Village Roots

The city calls me with neon eyes,
Tall buildings scrape,
the truth from skies,

But in my heart, a village sleeps,
With mustard fields and mango trees.

I walk in heels, I talk in codes,
But dreams still take those dusty roads,

Where evenings smell of burning hay,
And stars don't hide from light of day.

The world I chase is made of chrome,
Yet every win feels less like home.

And in the noise, my silence speaks—
A girl who misses river creeks.

8. Stars And Solitude

Lie under stars and close eyes,
Far from noise and city lies.

The sky doesn't rush, the wind's not loud,
It's just you and peace without a crowd.

you used to think you needed more,
But silence has a gentle core.

It hugs you in a way that stays,
Unlike people who drift in days.

Solitude isn't lonely or wrong,
It's where you go to feel strong.

Among the stars, you understand—
you are not alone. I just need my hand.

9. Nature Heals Quietly

There's a kind of calm in the trees,
A quiet language spoken by the breeze.

When the world gets too loud to bear,
I go where silence lives in air.

The sun doesn't judge, it simply shines,
The river flows without drawing lines.

Birds don't worry about the next day,
They just sing and fly away.

Nature reminds me I'm small,
But not worthless, not weak at all.

That life, like leaves, has seasons to go—
And after winter, flowers grow.

So I sit in the grass, close my eyes,
Let the clouds carry my cries.

Because sometimes, all I need to feel whole,

Is a sky to hold my soul.

10. Life Without Labels

She wasn't the topper, nor the best dressed,
Not first in line, nor like the rest.

She didn't know what path to choose,
Which dream to chase, what game to lose.

But slowly, softly, she began,
To live each day without a plan.

No title pinned upon her name,
No pressure to outshine or claim.

She found her joy in simple days,
In helping hands, in honest praise.

And bit by bit, without a prize—
She saw her life through kinder eyes.

Not all must roar to prove their place—
Some bloom in silence, full of grace.

11. That One Song

There's that one song you can't play,
Because it brings back that rainy day

.

The one where you both danced in dim light,
Where your eyes made the world feel right.

Now when you hear it, your chest tightens slow,
Like your heart remembers what you let go.

It plays in coffee shops, in cabs, in malls,
Like the universe whispers through its calls.

And though you have moved on, some part remains—
Trapped in that tune, tied to those chains.

Music holds memories no one can steal,
A hidden scar you will always feel.

12. Mirror Talk

You look in the mirror and fakes a grin,
Tries to see the beauty within.

But all you sees are flaws and doubt,
Whispers of "not enough" screaming out.

you compares yourself to every face,
Thinks you are last in this wild race.

But slowly you learns to soften that stare,
To treat yourself with gentle care.

you wipes the tears, stands tall again,
Tell your reflection, "You are not pain."

Day by day, you learn your worth—
Not from likes, or tags, or girth.

But from the truth that softly sings,
you are enough ,just as you brings.

13. Body
(Not a War Zone)

Your thighs are thick, your skin not clear,
But you refuse to shrink in fear.

You won't apologize for taking space,
Or hide your curves or change your face.

This body walks, this body feels,
It bears the pain, and slowly heals.

It's not for judgment, likes or fame,
It's your story, not your shame.

you are not broken, you are whole,
you won't trade size for someone's goal.

From your scars to stretch marks shown—
your body is not someones to own

14. A Little Light Called Hope

There's a candle in you, tiny but bright,
That flickers in every long, dark night.

When you feel like giving in or giving up,
Hope shows up in the smallest cup.

Sometimes it's just a stranger's smile,
Or your mom's call after a long while.

A song that knows just how you feel,
Or the way your wounds slowly heal.

Hope doesn't scream–
it whispers low,
It says, "Keep going,
you'll learn and grow."

Even when everything breaks apart,
It tucks itself in your beating heart.

So you will fall, cry,
maybe pause for a bit—
But you won't let that candle quit.

Because even when you don't feel whole—
Hope keeps breathing life in your soul.

15. Why Do We Outgrow People

You laughed until you cried that night,
Promised to hold on tight.

But somewhere between then and now,
You changed,
And you don't know how.

You liked silence,
They liked sound,
They wanted skies,
You stayed on ground.

You both used to share each tiny scar,
Now you wonder who you are.

Outgrowing people feels so strange,
Like flipping books you can't exchange.

But maybe growth means letting go,
Of things that no longer help you grow.

16. That Night

One night you sat with just your thoughts,
No music, no calls, no tangled knots.

you faced your fears, each hidden face,
And met yourself in a quiet place.

you wasn't loud, you wasn't bold,
you looked like stories never told.

With tired eyes and hopeful sighs,
A person who dared to still rise.

you talked like strangers, slow and deep,
Of wounds that fester, dreams that sleep.

And in gaze, you saw the truth–
you have been enough since your youth.

17. Not All Wounds Bleed

Some wounds don't bleed,
they ache in layers,
They hide in smiles and silent prayers.

They don't show up with broken skin,
But live in hearts we hold within.

The world may say,
"It wasn't much,"
But pain is pain–
It's in the touch.
It's in the flashbacks late at night,
It's in the way we dim our light.

But healing isn't some grand show,
It's crying soft where no one knows.
It's saying "no,"
It's sleeping deep,
It's learning boundaries we keep.

Some wounds don't bleed,
But still, they mend—
With time, with love, with one true friend.

18. A Garden Of You

You are not the not the person you used to be,
Soft-spoken shadow, quiet plea

you've bloomed through soil they thought too dry,
you've whispered no,
you’ve dared to try.

Some petals fell,
some roots grew deep,

Some lessons stung,
Some dreams lost sleep.

But here you stand, a little tall,
With scars that still remember all.

you watered wounds with silent tears,
And danced alone with changing years.

No, you are not perfect,

Neat or planned—
But still you grow,
Still you expand.

Each day, you bloom a little more—
A garden life was waiting for.

19. In Her Silence

She doesn't speak when thoughts run wild,
Her mind's a maze since she was a child.

She replays lines from years ago,
And wonders why she can't let go.

She says, "I'm fine," then overthinks,
Connects her flaws like missing links.

She's loud inside, but calm outside,
A storm in stillness she can't hide.

But in that silence lives her power,
She grows a garden, hour by hour.

Her thoughts may scream, but still she stands,
With anxious breath and trembling hands.

She may not quiet every fear,
But she survives, year after year.

20. To A Brown Girl

She's not the shade they paint in art,
But earth-toned fierce with golden heart.

They called her "too dark" in her youth,
But now she walks in deeper truth.

She's not ashamed of sun-kissed skin,
Her strength lies loud and proud within.

She wears her roots like woven gold,
In every word, her fire bold.

Not everyone may call her queen,
But she's the force behind the scene.

A brown girl rising, strong and real—
Her beauty's not for them to seal.

She's more than pretty, more than pride—
She is the storm they can't divide.

21. The Girl Who Observe

She's not the loudest in the room,
She'd rather watch the flowers bloom.

She sees the cracks beneath your grin,
She knows the war you hold within.

She doesn't speak just to be heard,
But when she does, she means each word.

She finds the beauty few will see—
In broken bark, in humble tea.

Some call her quiet, lost in haze,
But she just walks her own soft maze.

Not every light must blind or shout—
Some glow in corners,soft yet stout.

She's not unnoticed—just unseen.
But oh, the worlds she walks between.

22. Kept All Cards

You're the one who still remembers birthdays by heart,
Who keeps notes and tickets like they're pieces of art.

Your shelf holds dusty albums with scribbled names,
From friends who drifted, from childhood games.

You smiled like the past still danced in your room,
Like friendship could live after it met its doom.

You still send long texts just to check in,
Even when replies grow thinner, then thin.

You remember what people wore when they cried,
What song they hummed when someone died.

You don't let go, even when you should—
You believe in bonds like childhood wood.

Unpolished, scratched, but carved so deep,
That even time forgets to sweep.

If anyone forgets how to be a friend,
They should look at you and just pretend

They knew how to care that soft, that true—
The way you do, without needing a cue.

23. The Boy (His Tired Eyes At Bus Stop)

Every morning at six, he stands by the same pole,
Backpack slung low, eyes dark like coal.

His shoes are worn, soles peeling thin,
But his spine stays straight, carved from within.

He doesn't speak much, doesn't glance around,
Just watches the road, earphones drowned

Sometimes, a book peeks from his side,
Pages marked, corners fried.

He studies between stops, between sighs,
Between the noise and the sleepy skies.

There's fire in kids like him—slow and deep,
Burning silently while the world's asleep.

No trophies yet, no medals to show,
Just silent grit and a steady glow.

He may not know it, but he is the kind
That changes the course of a tired mind
.

Not with noise, or rage, or speed—
But with patience, hunger, and quiet need.

24. Still Learning

you used to think by this age,
Have all figured out.
But the truth is, every day still
Comes with its share of doubt.

Some days you feel powerful,
Like you can touch the sky.
Other days, you don't even want
To get up or try.

You make mistakes.
You say the wrong things.
Cry for reasons don't understand,
And get hurt by little things.

But that doesn't mean you are lost.
It just means you are still growing.
So if you're feeling behind,
Please don't think you're weak.

We all walk at our own pace,
And even the strong have weeks when they're meek.
Still learning, still falling,
But also still rising too.

And maybe that's what life really is—
Trying again, and again, until bloom.

25. Our Quietest Victory

It wasn't when we got the trophy,
Or when stood on stage.
Not even when they clapped for us,
Or printed name on a page.

Biggest win was much smaller,
No camera, no big crowd.
It was the day we didn't quit,
When everything felt too loud.

When we cried in the washroom,
But came back with steady eyes.
When we studied after failing,
And still chose not to lie.

The world may never know it,
May never call it success.
But to us, that silent stand
Was more than any test.

So when think of victories,
Don't count the medals or grade—
Count the days kept going,

26. Morning
(With Baba)

He didn't say much in words,
But his actions spoke loud.

Baba believed in small things—
Like polishing shoes, standing proud.

He'd make tea just right,
Not too sweet, not too strong,

And he'd place my cup beside his,
Like I'd been grown up all along.

Sometimes we sat in silence,
Just watching the street go by.

But those quiet morning hours
Taught me more than any why.

He told me how dreams need patience,

How respect is never loud.

And that even the smallest kindness
Could make someone feel proud.

27. Smell Of Maa
(Weight Stand Hand)

Her hands were always busy—
Rolling rotis, fixing hair,
Sewing buttons, holding books,
And wiping every little tear.

They weren't soft or painted,
But they told a story loud—
Of endless care and sacrifice,
Of love without any sound.

When we was sick, her hands cooled our head,
When we cried, they held us tight.
And when we won even the smallest prize,
Her claps made everything right.

Didn't notice them much before,
But now we miss them every day.
No spa, no cream, no gold
Can ever shine in that same way.

If heaven has a scent,
It's the smell of Maa's wheat-stained hand.
No poetry will ever be enough
To make the world understand.

28. Maa And Her Mirror

I once caught Maa looking in the mirror,
Tucking her grey hair behind her ear.
She smiled, but not like before,
As if time had whispered near.

I said, "You're still so beautiful, Maa,"
And she laughed, brushing it away.
"Beauty fades," she softly said,
"But love and work always stay."

But I don't think she knows at all,
How her eyes still shine so bright.
How the lines on her face
Tell stories of her fight.

She's the kind of beautiful
That never ages or breaks—
A beauty that cooks, prays, scolds,
And gives more than it takes.

So I wish she'd look again
And see what I always see—
A woman more glowing than any mirror,
Who built the best parts of me.

29. The Brother (Who Became Wall)

He never asked you what was wrong,
He just stood a little closer that day.
And when you didn't eat at dinner,
He kept your plate anyway.

He never liked loud feelings,
Never knew the right words to say.
But when life knocked you off balance,
He didn't let you drift away.

He guided you like traffic lights,
Quiet but always near.
He never let you feel alone,
Even when he wasn't here.

Now he's far, working late,
Busy building dreams of his own—
But his messages still come like clockwork:
"Reached home?" "Take care, phone!"

And you smile at that one line,
Because in it, you read it all—
That I'll always have a brother,
Who'll never let you fall.

30. Papa`s Wallet

Papa's wallet was never thick,
But it carried dreams galore.

Bills folded, photos tucked,
And love that asked for more.

Torn at the edges, stitched with care,
It held every penny tight.

He never bought shoes for himself,
But gave me books with pride.

Inside, I once found my report card—
The one I thought was small.

He carried it like a medal,
As if I had conquered all.

I asked him, "Why do you keep it still?"
He smiled and softly said,

"Every number you ever earned
Paid off the tears I shed."

31. A Dream Too Stubborn To Die

They told her it was foolish,
A castle made of air,

But she held it like a compass,
With a stubborn kind of care.

The world gave her a thousand ways
To quit and walk away,

But she stitched her hope with threads of steel,
And faced another day.

She didn't roar like revolution,
Or rise like breaking news,

But quietly, she chased the stars,
With nothing left to lose.

And now that dream is breathing,

Alive because she tried—

Proof that even softest dreams
Can live if not denied.

32. Not The Main Character

She's not the star in every tale,
Not the one they always choose,

She plays the role behind the scenes,
And often seems to lose.

But she's the one who listens,
The one who truly cares,

The one who finds the broken things
And mends them with her prayers.

You won't find her in headlines,
Or stories loud and grand,

But she's the silent strength you need,
When life gets out of hand.

Not all heroes wear the crown,
Or walk in spotlight's grace—

Some wear shadows on their sleeves,
And still, they find their place.

33. Her Name Wasn`t Mentioned

She's not the star in every tale,
Not the one they always choose,

She plays the role behind the scenes,
And often seems to lose.

But she's the one who listens,
The one who truly cares,

The one who finds the broken things
And mends them with her prayers.

You won't find her in headlines,
Or stories loud and grand,

But she's the silent strength you need,
When life gets out of hand.

Not all heroes wear the crown,

Or walk in spotlight's grace—

Some wear shadows on their sleeves,
And still, they find their place.

34. The Sound Of Hope

It doesn't roar like thunder,
Or dazzle like the stars,

Hope is quiet, soft, and gentle—
It heals our deepest scars.

It comes in tiny moments,
In coffee on cold days,

In a message from a friend
When you're lost in life's maze.

Hope doesn't need a spotlight,
It lives where few can see,

In a whisper, in a heartbeat,
In the strength to simply be.

It doesn't promise magic,
Or that you'll never fall—

But it will walk beside you,
When you've got nothing at all.

35. The Life You Never Posted

I wish you saw the moments
You never dared to share,
Not filtered into colors,
Or posed with perfect hair.

The night you broke but held it in,
The smile wore with pain,
The times you laughed through heartbreak,
And danced inside the rain.

they saw the curated snapshots,
The highlights you allowed,
But not the dreams you buried deep
To fit into the crowd
.

you posted joy in pixels,
But hid your fear in drafts,
You saw the wins, the travels,
Not the lonely aftermaths.

Yet still, you have grown in silence,
In spaces out of frame,
And every scar you carry now
Still speaks your burning flame.

So maybe you won't know it all,
The storms you have walked alone—
But trust me when I say this life
Is more than what is shown.

36. The Boy And His Self Doubt

He looked strong from the outside,
His stride calm, firm, and neat—

But every step he ever took
Felt fragile underneath.

They called him brave, intelligent,
A boy who had it all—

But no one saw the tiny cracks
That led him close to fall.

He smiled when praised, but questioned it,
"Am I really enough?"

Behind his jokes and clever lines,
He found believing tough.

He's learning now to trust his light,

To not dim for the crowd—

Even boys with shining eyes
Can wrestle with their doubt.

37. He Never Sent (That Letters)

He writes in his notes app,
But never hits send,

Messages for a lover,
Or a long-lost friend.

He pours his heart in silence,
Hopes someone might reply–

But fear ties up his fingers
And leaves him wondering why.

Some boys don't speak in poems,
They hide them in their phone–

Waiting for a moment
They never truly own.

38. He And His Bike

It wasn't just a ride for him,
It was his great escape—

From lectures, fights, and expectations
He could no longer shape.

The road became his closest friend,
The wind, his only guide,

And though the world kept asking more,
He found his truth in rides.

He wasn't lost or reckless,
Just craving something free—

And every time ,
He kicked that start,
He felt who he could be.

39. The Friend Who Stayed

When everyone walked out the door,
And silence filled her days,

There was one who didn't ask for much—
Just sat beside the haze.

No advice, no sugar lines,
No lectures dressed as care—

Just presence like a steady light
That told you, "I am there."

They laughed without a reason,
They cried without regret—

Some bonds don't need explaining,
They're just the safest bet.

Not all angels come with wings,
Some wear a friend's old tee—

And show up when the world forgets
Who you were born to be.

40. Her First Job

She stepped into the office door
With dreams tucked in her bag,

Her shoes a little worn with hope,
Her skirt a little sagged

.

She smiled through mispronounced replies,
She learned to take the lead—

With shaky hands but steady eyes,
She taught herself to lead.

No one saw the late-night tears
Or how she doubted still,

But every paycheck in her hand
Was more than just a bill.

41. First Love
(On Lat Bench)

He sat two rows behind her,
In lectures she forgot,

Yet somehow every fleeting glance
Left her stomach in a knot.

They never shared more than a smile,
A borrowed pen, a joke–

But in that tiny corner seat,
A gentle love awoke.

They walked out as strangers
When college came to close,

But she still thinks of him sometimes
In poems no one knows.

For some love stories never start,

Yet live like they began—

She loved him in her silence,
And maybe, so did he in his plan.

42. The Introvert (In The Corner)

You never led the group chats loud,
Or stormed into the scene—

you sat beside the windowsill
And watched the sky turn green.

you didn't say too much in class,
Avoided every stage—

But wrote the world in bullet points
Across your journal's page.

They called you shy, invisible,
But never really knew—

you held galaxies inside her head
And oceans in your view.

Some voices aren't the loudest ones,

But echo through the years—

Like yours, a soft and steady hum
That overcomes all fears.

43. Mind That Never Sleeps

You turns off every single light,
The clock says 3:04–

But your mind plays reels of "what ifs"
You lived a thousand more.

A text you sent last week replays,
A look you misread wrong–

And every breath becomes a task
That doesn't feel too strong.

They say just breathe, just let things go,
Just trust the path ahead–

But they don't know the weight of thoughts
That rattle in your head.

Still you wakes and ties her hair,
Smiles though you are not fine–

And fights a war no one can see
One breath at a time.

44. Missed Calls, Missed Chance

He stared at the last missed call,
The one he didn't take–

he thought he would call her back next day,
But life doesn't always wait.

They grew apart like drifting boats
That once had shared the shore–

And now they only meet in dreams
Or songs they both adore.

he wonders if she thinks of him,
If she still hums that song–

If silence ever aches for her
The way it does so long.

Some goodbyes never said aloud

Still echo in your chest—

And leave behind a quiet space
Where “almost” comes to rest.

45. Heavy Eyes

He laughs in group chats, cracks a joke,
And always says, "I'm cool,"

But walks alone the longest way
Back home from evening school.

He's tired, but he'll never say—
He's trained to hold it in,

Because they told him, "Boys don't cry,"
Since he was ten or ten.

He lifts the weight of family dreams,
Pretends he's doing great—

But even courage starts to bend
When hearts accumulate.

So if you see him lost in thought,
Don't ask him to be tough—

Just sit and say, "I see your fight—
And yes, you are enough."

46. Hostel Room 208

Three girls shared a single room,
With fights and Maggie bowls,

Late-night talks and crying spells,
And dreams with open goals.

Notes scattered on the study desk,
A diary no one read—

One danced to heartbreak songs at night,
One barely left her bed.

They promised they would never part,
That college wouldn't end—

But now they text just once a month,
A meme, or "Hey there, friend."

Yet every time she smells that soap,
Or sees a steel plate shine—

She's back in Room 208,
With girls she called divine.

47. Just Another Monday

Rushing with books and tangled hair,
Running behind a bus, half-aware,

A toast half-burnt, a dream half-spun,
A life in motion, a race not won.

you sits in class with tired eyes,
Yet fights to learn, to memorize.

your world's too big for rules that bind,
you are chasing stars with a stubborn mind.

And though the week feels long and gray,
you still believes in a brighter day.

So here you go, not seeking fame–
Just another Monday, just the same.

48. Letters

In a drawer of thoughts, they lie unread,
All the words you never said.

Pages folded with silent screams,
Sealed in ink and broken dreams.

One was for a friend you lost,
Another for love, no matter the cost.

Some were poems, some were prayers,
Some just asked if someone cares.

you never mailed them, never dared,
But writing them made you feel less scared

For in those letters, you became—
The person who wrote but never blamed.

49. Cafe Corner

There's a table near the window seat,
Where dreams and deadlines always meet.

Old wooden chairs, a dusty shelf,
A place where I can just be myself.

We'd sit there laughing after class,
With half-done notes and empty glass.

The chai was cheap, the mood was gold,
And stories spilled that stayed untold.

He came one day, all shy and late,
Our hands brushed close—was it just fate?

He quoted poems, I rolled my eyes,
But smiled inside and felt surprise.

Now months have passed, the café's changed,
Our friend group scattered, all estranged.

But I return and find my seat,
Where heart and memory always meet.

The café corner whispers low,
Of first hellos and last goodbyes so slow.

50. Tea Stall Dairy

The kettle sings its smoky tune,
Beside a tired afternoon.

At roadside stalls with plastic cups,
The world slows down, then opens up.

A rickshaw puller, shirt half-torn,
Talks politics with college-born.

Two lovers sit, their fingers near,
Not touching, but the silence clear.

The chai-wallah knows every face,
Knows who's in love, who lost the race.

He pours his wisdom sip by sip,
With every brew, life starts to slip.

No five-star table, shining bright—
Just benches lit by yellow light.

Yet hearts are healed and words are made
Over hot tea and dreams delayed.

This is no café, no grand escape—
Just paper cups and real-life shape.

51. Girl In The Red Kurti

She wasn't the loudest in the room,
Nor did she carry scent or bloom.
But something in her made you stay—
A calm that pulled the noise away.

She wore a red kurti that swayed,
With anklets soft, her charm unplayed.
No smoky eyes, no sharpened line,
Yet in her eyes, the stars would shine.

She didn't flirt, didn't pretend,
But always asked how days would end.
Her laugh was rare, but when it came—
It lit the air, like wild flame.

Boys would wonder what it was,
That made them pause, rethink, because—
She wasn't trying to impress,
But somehow made their world feel less.

And in that red, she'd pass you by,
Not knowing hearts were asking why—
The simplest girl could leave such trace,
With just her soul and gentle grace.

52. Boy's Do Write Poem

He sat three benches to my right,
Kept doodling lines in dim twilight
.Not football stats or brand new tech—
But stanzas scrawled across his desk.

He'd tear the pages, blush and hide,
Like poems weren't made for a boy's pride.
Yet in those words, raw truths would flow—
Of love, of fear, of letting go.

He wrote of moms who worked too late,
Of fathers burdened by their fate.
Of nights he cried into his sleeve,
And mornings masked by make-believe.

The world taught him to be a man,
To lead, to fight, to never stand
In front of mirrors filled with doubt—
To never let the soft come out.

But still he wrote, though none could see,
His poems bled out quietly.
Boys don't write poems, people say—
But I've seen one, and he's okay.

53. Library Girl

She walks in quiet, finds her place,
Behind the shelves, she hides her face.

A world too loud, too fast to feel–
She turns to books to help her heal.

She's marked each page with dreams and ink,
The stories say what she can't think

.

She reads of wars, of stars that fall,
Of women rising after all.

While others chase the trending scene,
She lives in lands they've never seen.

A rebel not with swords, but pens,
She makes her own beginnings, ends.

They say she's shy, they never knew–
The fire in her pages grew.

She's not the girl who speaks aloud,
But in her silence, she stands proud.

So if you pass her, smile and see—
The Library Girl is wild and free.

54. The Unpopular Girl

She sat alone on every bench,
Her voice too soft, her look too French.

She didn't wear the latest trend,
But carried stories none could bend.

They whispered names, they made her small,
But still she walked, still stood tall.

For in her silence, worlds would bloom,
In notebooks hidden in her room.

She wasn't made for glitter lights,
Or gossip wars or Friday nights.

Yet in her eyes, you'd find the moon—
A depth that spoke in quiet tune.

One day, they'll search her in a book,
In lines they once refused to look

And they will learn what they ignored—
That magic doesn't need applause or sword.

The unpopular girl they used to tease,
Will rise with words and write with ease.

55. His Name Wasn`t In Headline

He didn't win a medal bright,
Or stand beneath a camera light.

No one clapped when she passed by,
But still, he fought and learned to fly.

He worked part-time, skipped his lunch,
But never lost his hopeful hunch.

While others chased applause and fame,
He whispered goals, lit up her flame.

And though his hands were rough and sore,
His mind kept building something more.

No trophy shelf, no viral post,
Just little wins he loved the most.

Like paying fees, or learning math,

Or walking proud his own new path.

They may not know the life he made,
But strength like his will never fade.

His name's not carved on silver plates,
But written deep in future's gates.

56. Page From His Dairy

He never spoke of love out loud,
wasn't built for every crowd.

But in his room, each night at nine,
He poured herself in every line.

A diary hidden, locked with care,
Its pages worn from nightly wear.

He wrote of friends who didn't stay,
Of dreams that begged to find a way.

He spoke to stars through paper sheets,
Of rainy walks and lonely streets.

He cried in ink, then smiled again,
A cycle sweet of joy and pain.

He wrote of her, of how he smiled,
Of how her heart would run so wild.

Of words he wished he dared to say—
But only dared to write each day.

The world may never know his truth,
But those torn pages hold his youth.

A thousand lives he chose to live—
In words only the night could give.

57. Her Type

He wasn't tall, or rich, or wild,
He didn't drive the girls beguiled.

He never flirted, never played,
His shirts were plain, his hair unlaid.

Yet somehow, she looked back one day,
And saw the sun behind the gray.

He held a book, not beer or pride,
And walked with peace the world denied.

He didn't say, "You look divine,"
But asked, "Are you truly doing fine?"

And she, who'd laughed at boys like him,
Found her heart beginning to dim.

He brought her chai, not fancy wine,
He noticed silence, gave her time.

And though he wasn't "her type," she knew—
The truest hearts wear the plainest hue.

58. Midnight Thought (In Hostel Room)

The fan spins slow in midnight air,
The walls still echo laughter there.

Roommates lie in scattered dreams,
While you lie wide with silent screams.

A diary's open by your bed,
A hundred thoughts, a thousand said.

From fights with friends to calls grown cold,
To fears you barely want to hold.

The hostel buzzes, dim and low,
Outside, the world begins to slow.

But in your mind, it's loud and wild,
The warrior heart of a sleepless child.

you miss your home, the food, the sound,

The love that never had to be found.

But you are here, alone, not weak—
you will learn to fight and find what you seek.

Because someday soon, this room, this night,
Will be the root of all your flight.

59. People Who Leaves Quietly

They don't shout, they don't explain,
They pack their peace and take their pain.

No long goodbyes, no final texts—
Just distance built with silent steps.

You think they're fine, they always smile,
But they've been hurting all the while.

They give and give until they break,
Then gather pieces no one takes.

You search for them a week too late,
By then, they've locked another gate.

Their presence fades like morning mist,
A chapter lost, a name dismissed.

Yet sometimes in a crowd, you'll see—

A laugh that sounds like who they'd be.

And then you'll know, and it'll sting—
Quiet goodbyes are a lifelong thing.

60. When Nobody Text First

You wait a while, then wait some more,
You glance again at that closed door.

You type a 'Hi' but hit delete,
Convinced the silence is concrete.

You tell yourself it's not that deep,
Then cry alone before you sleep

.

Because love that fades without a fight,
Isn't a loss–it's theft at night.

Friendships too can drift away,
With unspoken things we couldn't say.

And pride becomes a heavy wall,
We'd rather wait than make that call.

But deep inside, the ache is loud–
We miss the laughs, the noisy crowd.

Yet no one moves, no one forgives,
And in that stillness, distance lives.

So here you are, heart unrehearsed,
Stuck in the war of "Who texts first?

61. Evening On The Rooftop

When books are closed and dinner's done,
We all climbs upstairs to meet the sun.

A little rooftop, cracked and bare,
Becomes our kingdom in the air.

We spreads a mat, our journal too,
While twilight paints the sky with blue.

We listens not to noisy phones,
But whispering winds and flying drones.

The city hums below our feet,
But here, our soul finds its heartbeat.

We watches stars begin to wake,
And feels the world begin to break.

From here,we dream without a lid,
Of things we lost and things we did.

The sky becomes our open page,
Where fear dissolves and thoughts engage.

In crowded towns and hectic days,
The rooftop is our quiet place.

62. Friend Who Left (Without Goodbye)

We shared our lunch, our fears, our skin,
Our jokes, our secrets tucked within.

We stayed up late, we talked for hours,
We named our dreams and drew them flowers.

But time, it changed the lines we drew,
And suddenly, I lost you too.

No fight, no blame, no bitter end–
Just silence where there was a friend.

I searched old chats and pictures framed,
Still whispered softly your sweet name.

But life had plans we couldn't hold,
And stories left untold grew cold.

I hope you're laughing, doing fine,

Chasing sunsets that once were mine.

Though distance stretched across the sky,
You left too soon, without goodbye.

Still, in my mind, we talk sometimes—
In shared old songs and nursery rhymes.

63. When You Miss Someone (Who Is Alive)

It's strange to miss a living soul,
Like holding air you can't control.

They're breathing still, and laugh out loud,
But not for you, not in your crowd.

You see them post, they seem just fine,
While you reread the warning sign.

They walk this Earth, as strangers do,
Though once they knew the deepest you.

You check their name, then scroll away,
Pretending that you're okay each day.

But grief for someone still around–
Is lonelier than burial ground.

You hold your tongue, you hide your tears,
You drown in "what ifs" through the years.

And though you live, and love again—
A part of you still speaks their name.

Some losses wear a beating heart,
And hurt the most while worlds restart.

64. Late NIght Before Exam

The books are open, snacks nearby,
The clock ticks loud beneath the sky.

She flips through notes with weary eyes,
As formulas blur and focus dies.

There's coffee stains on chapter three,
And doodles where graphs used to be.

Her room's a mess, her bun is high–
Her courage held, though tears run dry.

She whispers mnemonics in a chant,
"I will remember... no, I can't."

But still she reads, and scribbles fast,
As sunrise dares to rise at last.

No magic wand, no lucky charm,
Just calloused hands and aching arm.

And though the world may never know—
Her battle lives in that faint glow.

For every rank begins somewhere—
In late night rooms with scattered hair.

65. Sunday Feels Like Home

There's something in the Sunday air–
The lazy sky, the sun's soft stare.

A chai in hand, a messy braid,
Old songs in corners gently played.

The world moves slow, without a race,
And peace peeks through each empty space.

Mom's voice hums from another room,
The floor is swept, the flowers bloom.

The TV plays a film halfway,
While dad reads news and slips away.

No urgent texts, no time to chase,
Just silence smiling face to face.

Some Sundays feel like childhood breeze–
Of mango slices, rustling trees.

They hold us close, and gently say—
"You're growing up, but you can stay."

And even when the Monday calls,
That Sunday sun still softly falls.

66. What If Never Get Their

What if you climb and still don't win?
What if success won't let you in?

What if the doors all stay shut tight,
And you just fade from every light?

What if the crowd forgets your name?
And hard work leaves you just the same?

These thoughts don't knock, they barge right through,
On sleepless nights and mornings blue.

But still, you try, despite the storm,
With trembling hands that don't perform.

For maybe dreams aren't made to please,
But keep us walking on our knees.

And even if you fail to rise—
At least you reached beyond the skies.

67. Cafeteria Table Knows It All

The corner table, sticky top,
Has seen more tales than it could mop.

Of crushes told with trembling spoon,
Of breakups crying into noon.

It holds the laughter, holds the tea,
The spilled out secrets casually.

It's where she stared while he looked down,
And where a friend first fixed her crown.

Some carved their names into the wood,
Some just sat longer than they should.

A chai was shared, a fight forgot,
A joke that made a sad day hot.

Now students change and chairs do too,

But tables keep what people rue.

They age in silence, scratched and scarred,
But hold your heart like greeting card.

A place where youth and dreams collide—
And memories wait on either side.

68. Last Bench ,Last Day

The chalk dust swirled in morning sun,
The bell rang out, the year was done.

They packed their bags, but took too long—
As if goodbye could be so strong.

The last bench held their names in ink,
The secrets only wood could think.

The jokes they passed, the notes they threw,
The silent crushes no one knew.

One looked around, then softly said,
"Remember when we painted red?"

Another smiled, and bit her lip—
Recalling every failed test slip.

They clicked a pic, half tears, half grin,
With time already pulling in.

And though they'd go their different way,
The last bench wouldn't fade away.

It holds the end, the sweet and sore—
Of school days they will live no more.

69. Half Burnt

She found them in a rusted box,
Tied in threads and covered locks.

Letters half-burnt, yet words remained,
Of someone once, who loved, then pained.

Some smelled of ink, some stained by rain,
Some whispered laughter, some moaned pain.

They didn't end in final lines—
Just faded hope in crooked signs.

One said, "I'll wait," but didn't last,
Another, "Sorry," from the past.

She held them close, then held her chest,
As memories pulled her from rest.

She didn't cry, nor curse the name—
Just smiled, for love that never came.

Not every tale needs perfect close—
Some hearts grow strong from what they chose.

She lit a match, let paper fly,
And watched old ghosts float to the sky.

70. Jon Interview And Coffee Breath

She wore her dreams in borrowed shoes,
A blazer tight, yet full of views.

The waiting room smelled faint of sweat,
Of nervous hearts and cold regret.

She clutched her file, rehearsed her part,
“Good morning, sir” with thumping heart.

Beside her sat a boy as tense,
Both betting on their common sense.

Inside, the clock moved slow and sharp,
The AC hummed like a broken harp.

And though she’d dreamed of chairs and pay,
She now just hoped for light that day.

Not every dream comes dressed in gold—
Some knock in rooms just barely bold.

71. He Let Other Win

He'd pass the ball, avoid the race,
Step back to let another place.

He cheered the loudest from the side,
While holding storms he'd never confide.

He'd smile when others took the prize,
Though sadness clouded in his eyes.

They called him kind, the selfless friend,
Not knowing where his wishes end.

He gave his seat, he gave his turn,
And hid the fire he'd let burn.

But kindness isn't just a trait—
It's often love dressed up as wait.

And one fine day, he chose to stand,
To raise his voice, to raise his hand.

He played the game, he wrote his name,
No longer lost in someone's flame.

Because the ones who always give—
Deserve their moment too, to live.

72. Almost Their

They said, "You're almost there," with half a smile,
As if 'almost' could stretch across a mile.
As if 'almost' was a victory song,
Instead of a road that feels too long.

You sat on benches of near-success,
Wearing a crown of second-best,
Watching trains pass with blinking signs,
Carrying faces that weren't yours.

You measured my worth in broken clocks,
In calls unanswered, in unopened locks.
They said, "Try harder," like you hadn't bled,
Like your dreams weren't stitched in red.

you carried books heavier than your fears,
Carried hope through whispered sneers,
You drank bitterness in silver cups,
And still found strength to stand up.

They called you resilient, like it was a prize,
When all you did was refuse their lies.
Almost there? Almost won?
Maybe almost is where legends are spun.
Because standing at the edge, and bare,

73. Roots And Wings

They gave me roots, sturdy and deep,
Tales of patience, promises to keep.
But I wanted wings – wild and wide,
To chase the winds they learned to hide.

I loved the soil, the steady ground,
But craved the sky's uncharted sound.
Roots held me tight when storms would shout,
Wings whispered dreams I couldn't live without.

Torn between earth and endless skies,
I chose to fall, I chose to rise.
With every wound, with every scar,
I flew closer to my stubborn star.

Roots reminded me where I began,
Wings taught me what I truly am.
And now – wherever fate may swing,
I bless my roots, but I wear my wings.

74. Seasons Of Friendship

Friendships are not built in sunny days,
They're stitched in storms, in messy ways.
They grow in crowded college halls,
In late-night talks and drunken calls.

They fade and fall and bloom again,
Like seasons lost inside our veins.
Some friends stay – loyal and true,
Some leave when the sky turns blue.

Friendship is laughter inside a crowded train,
A tear wiped off without explaining the pain.
It's borrowed sweaters, endless memes,
It's whispered failures and loud dreams.

Years will pass, some faces will blur,
But a true friend's memory will always stir.
Like autumn leaves inside an old book,
You'll find them – if you know where to look.

75. Girl Who Stayed

She stayed when the storms begged her to run,
She stayed when the battles were never won.
Not because she didn't know the way out,
But because she believed in her own shout.

She built castles with broken stones,
Sang lullabies over cracked bones.
Wrote poems with bleeding hands,
Turned scars into golden bands.

She stayed when it was easier to leave,
Planted gardens where she couldn't breathe.
Painted walls over wounds unseen,
Wore her pain in shades of green.

Not every hero wears a cape,
Some just refuse to escape.
She stayed – and that was her song,
The softest heart
With the loudest, fiercest song.

76. Messy Art Of Growing Up

No one tells you growing up is this messy,
Like rain on laundry or kisses too hasty.
One day you're sure – the next, you fall,
One step forward, two into a wall.

You outgrow rooms, clothes, even friends,
Mend some dreams, and break some ends.
You find your voice just as it cracks,
Build new bridges on old train tracks.

Growing up isn't clean or bright,
It's midnight calls and silent fights.
It's loving yourself through awkward tries,
It's stitching strength where weakness lies.

No certificate, no golden prize,
Just quiet mornings and braver eyes.
Growing up is falling – and still believing

That getting back up
Is its own kind of living.

77. Wandere's Heart

The road calls louder than the clocks,
The hills hum songs through weathered rocks.
Maps crumpled in the backseat pile,
Dreams drawn in every wandering mile.

I carry no compass, no fixed plan,
Just shoes worn out by places I ran.
Cities, villages, broken towers,
Sleepless trains, sunburnt hours.

I collect sunsets, not souvenirs,
I count laughter, not the years.
No home but the open sky,
No goodbye that truly says goodbye.

A wanderer's heart is stitched in flight,
Always searching, never quite right.
Because some souls aren't made to stay,
They find themselves
Along the way.

78. Golden Afternoon

Golden afternoons wrapped in dust,
Paper boats floating on puddle crust.

Sticky candies, scraped-up knees,
Secret forts built under neem trees.

Stories invented on cracked front steps,
Dreams spinning with every breath.

The world was ours, vast and wide,
Fitting into pockets where we used to hide.

No deadlines, no farewells, no maps,
Just dreams embroidered into midday naps.

If I close my eyes, I can still find,
That golden afternoon inside my mind.

79. The Choice

You chose yourself today,
In a world that begs you to sway.

To fold, to shrink, to dim your glow,
You stood taller and said, "No."

You chose the road that wasn't straight,
The path that questioned every fate.

You chose mistakes over silent fear,
You chose to stay – even when unclear.

In choosing myself, you lost a few,
But those who matter always knew.

Sometimes winning means walking alone,
Sometimes freedom feels like home.

80. The Last Bell Rings

The last bell rings – and silence falls,
Empty chairs, deserted halls.

Half-packed bags, tear-stained cheeks,
Promises rushed in parting speaks.

Dreams that once fit on a single page,
Now stretch toward an unwritten stage.

The canteen jokes, the library naps,
Are stitched forever in memory's maps.

We leave behind walls that held our fears,
Take forward laughter brewed through years.

And even as the world swings wide,
College days stay locked inside –

A dusty album, a golden song,
That calls us home when life feels wrong.

81. Forgiveness Is A Door

Forgiveness isn't a ribboned gift,
It's a slow, painful, uncertain shift.
It's not for them – it's for you alone,
To drop the sword, to leave the stone.

It's standing at the edge of rage,
And choosing to turn another page.
Not because they deserve the grace,
But because you deserve empty space.

It's the key to an invisible chain,
The shelter you build after the rain.
It's not forgetting – no, never that,
It's just refusing to wear their debt.

Forgiveness isn't saying it didn't scar –
It's saying the scar
Will no longer define who you are.

82. The Echo Of Failure

Failure echoes longer than fame,
Whispering doubts inside your name.

It carves shadows in your chest,
Turns simple steps into cruel tests.

But failure, too, is a kind of art,
The breaking that strengthens the heart.

The unfinished song, the missed flight,
The wrong choices made in desperate night.

Each fall rewrites your crooked map,
Each scar tightens your soul's strap.

And even when you think you're through,
Failure is only making room
For a stronger you.

83. The First Love Letter

It wasn't perfect, not even close,
Folded wrong with too much prose.

Ink smudged by sweaty palms,
Words wrapped up in nervous psalms.

You spelled forever with shaky hands,
Promised sunsets, wedding bands.

No fancy gifts, no stolen kiss,
Just shy hopes and foolish bliss.

It wasn't love as books might tell,
It was truer – clumsy, pure as well.

The first love letter never gets it right,
But oh,
It burns the brightest light.

84. The Art Of Running Away

Running away isn't always defeat,
Sometimes it's saving your own heartbeat.

Leaving rooms that drain your soul,
Escaping cages you didn't enroll.

It's the courage to say "not this,"
To step into shadows chasing bliss.

Running isn't cowardice or crime –
It's reclaiming your stolen time.

So pack your fears into a bag,
Shed your past like a tattered flag.

Sometimes running away
Is the only way
To truly stay.

85. Borrowed Joy

Happiness is not some distant land,
Not a prize you earn with perfect plans.

It's borrowed joy – in sudden beams,
In old songs, in forgotten dreams.

It's mango juice dripping down your chin,
It's laughing too loud, letting life win.

It's broken swings and barefoot sprints,
Finding poetry in subway hints.

Borrow joy where you can,
In strangers, dogs, skies and sand.

You don't need to own happiness outright –
Sometimes it's enough
Just to borrow the light.

86. Mask Of Perfect Love

We wear masks of perfect love,
Perfect smiles, perfect words from above.

But true love isn't flawless,
It's the broken pieces we proudly confess.

It's not always butterflies or wine,
Sometimes it's grief tangled with wine.

It's arguing till dawn, then making amends,
It's holding tight when the world bends.

The mask may shine, but the truth is clear —
Real love isn't perfect,
It's the mess you hold near.

87. Dancing With Time

Time is not a friend, nor foe,
It's a dancer, spinning slow.

We are partners in this fleeting waltz,
Taking steps in uncertain stalls.

It never waits, never bends,
Yet, it teaches the art of making amends.

We chase it, but it slips our grasp,
A fleeting shadow, a forgotten gasp.

So we dance with time, step by step,
Not knowing where the rhythm will let.

But we keep moving, through all the doubt,
Because even in chaos,
We don't sit out.

88. The Courage Of (Being Different)

The world will tell you to fit in line,
To be like others, and be just fine.

But you are the puzzle piece that doesn't blend,
A fire that refuses to descend.

There's beauty in being the one who stands,
The rebel with untamed hands.

You don't need to follow the mold,
When you're the one who dares to hold

The flame that others may not see,
But that's what makes you, you,

So free.
So wear your difference, wear it proud,
For the loudest voices
Are the ones unbowed.

89. Burden Of Expectation

We wear the weight of the world each day,
The pressures they say we must obey.

Chasing ideals, running too fast,
Living for the future, not the past.

They tell us to fit, to mold, to be,
But we are more than what they see.

We break under the weight of their hands,
Forcing us into boxes, like grains of sand.

But inside, we hold the strength to fight,
To break free, to take flight.

We don't need to be their dream,
We are the hope in the unseen.

90. Love That Needed No Witness

She loved him in a way, The world would never
understand,
Not in loud promises,But in silent folded hands.

Every morning, barefoot,she walked to the temple gate,
Carrying prayers heavier,Than the books she had to face.

He rose high, chasing skies,And somewhere lost his way,
She stayed behind, with tear-soaked nights,
Still wishing him brighter days.

When he confessed,she already knew –
Her heart had whispered,Long before he drew.

She said nothing,Not a word, not a sigh,
Just walked away,Letting silence cry.

There were hands,Stronger, richer than his,
But her soul never learned,To trade love like this.

But if someday he sees,Beyond applause,beyond noise-
And maybe one distant night ,when ego lost it's shine

He will look up at stars,find her name,
Written their ,brighter than all victories combined.

He might remember, their once was girl
who prayed for him
When he didn't even know he needed saving.

91. The Destiny

Some say destiny is a stubborn road,
A prewritten script in heavy code.

But I believe it's a living thing,
A compass dancing on a moving string.

Each choice a curve, each hope a turn,
Each broken bridge another learn.

Destiny isn't locked in stars –
It's scribbled between all your scars.

So hold your map with shaking hands,
Draw new countries, name new lands.

The compass only points;
You carve the way.

92. The God I Know

The God I know doesn't live behind rituals,
Or demand perfect prayers from trembling mouths.
He walks beside me in muddy shoes,
In broken dreams, unanswered nights,
And pages where my handwriting shakes.

He's in the soft voice that says,
"Try again,"
Even when I have no strength left to move.
He doesn't test me to see if I'll break,
He tests me to remind me
That I won't.

The God I know sends lessons in loss,
And strength in silence.
He answers, sometimes, with a delay
So I learn to trust not the timing,
But the love behind it.

He is not far—never was.

He hides in moments we don't photograph,
In the comfort of an old song,
In a stranger's unexpected kindness.
And when the world turns its back,
He still holds mine.

93. The Sacred Wait

What if waiting wasn't punishment,
But preparation?
What if unanswered prayers were just
Seeds still rooting under the soil?

We beg for doors to open,
But destiny walks slow,
It arrives when we've become the version
Of ourselves who can hold the weight of the blessing.

The sacred wait is not empty—
It's filled with learning,
With stretching, with surrender.
It's the space where faith grows teeth,
And belief stops needing proof.

When the world rushes ahead,
And your steps feel small—
Pause.
Because even paused journeys are protected

By something greater.

And when it's time—truly time—
Not even the strongest storm
Can keep it from reaching you.

94. A Path Already Known

I've walked roads I didn't choose,
Made peace with turns I never prayed for.
And still, somehow,
I arrived at places that felt like home.

Maybe that's what destiny is—
Not a straight line to glory,
But a thousand little moments
Of divine redirection.

We plan with calendars and alarms,
But God works in eternity.
He closes doors not to punish us,
But to shield us from rooms we don't belong in.

There's a path already known,
Woven in love before we were born.
Our task isn't to control it—
It's to trust it.

And when the day comes
Where everything makes sense,
We'll look back and smile,
Realizing we were never lost—
Only guided.

95. The God Within

You searched temples and stars,
Mountains and holy rivers,
For a glimpse of the Divine.
lit lamps, chanted names,
Offered coins and flowers.

But you never found peace
Until you closed your eyes,
And dared to sit with myself.

There, in the breath you ignored,
In the scars you tried to hide—
He lived.
Not far.
Not above.
Within.

The God within doesn't wear robes,
Doesn't demand ceremonies.
He speaks in intuition,

In dreams too wild to ignore.
He shows up in courage you didn't know you had,
And in tears that taught you strength.

you no longer search outside—
you carry Him,
And that has changed everything.

96. Destiny Never Forgets

There were years I felt forgotten—
Like my name had slipped
From the pages of the universe.
Everyone else seemed to bloom,
While I waited in quiet soil.

But destiny is not a train
That leaves without you.
It is a river—patient, persistent,
It bends to reach you,
Even if the world tells you
You've missed your chance.

It doesn't knock like opportunity—
It grows like dawn,
Soft and certain.

When it came,
It didn't come loud,
It came as peace.

Not a reward,
But a reminder—
That nothing meant for me
Will ever pass me by.

Because even when I gave up on me,
God didn't.

97. The Map You Cannot See

You make plans,
And life rearranges them—
Like winds blowing papers
Across a quiet room.
What you wanted last year
No longer fits this heart.

But you trust now,
That there's a map you cannot see,
Drawn in invisible ink,
Guided by hands that know better.

Every delay was a shield.
Every heartbreak—an initiation.
you didn't lose time,
you gained depth.

And the roads you feared
Were often detours
To something softer, truer,

Something only God could have drawn.

So now, you walk—not fast,
But full of faith.
Even when you don't know the way,
you know who draws it.

98. Written In Sky

Some say destiny is written in stars,
But I believe it's written in our becoming.
In the way we grow through grief,
In the way our scars begin to shine
Like constellations of survival.

You are not late.
You are not lost.
You are arriving—
Every heartbreak, a compass.
Every pause, a step forward
In a language only time can read.

The universe isn't pushing you—
It's unfolding for you.
Like petals that bloom when they're ready,
Like rivers that reach the sea
No matter how many rocks they touch.

Your story is not a mistake.

It is sacred—

And the stars?

They already know your name.

9 789370 923881

Printed by Libri Plureos GmbH in Hamburg,
Germany

Printed by Libri Plureos GmbH in Hamburg,
Germany